Isn't it Funny?

Riham Abusabha

Isn't it Funny? © 2023 Riham Abusabha

All rights reserved.

No part of this publication may be reproduced, stored in a retrieval system, or transmitted, in any form or by any means, electronic, mechanical, photocopying, recording or otherwise, without the prior written permission of the presenters.

Riham Abusabha asserts the moral right to be identified as author of this work.

Presentation by *BookLeaf Publishing*

Web: www.bookleafpub.com

E-mail: info@bookleafpub.com

ISBN: 9789357696647

First edition 2023

DEDICATION

I dedicate this book to those that possess the ability to understand the irony.

PREFACE

These poems exist to mock the current state of the world. Isn't it funny?

Manners of Contortion

Isn't it funny…

How the Western man claims
to fight for women's rights.
All while completely disregarding
a woman's plights.
They assume their delusional roles
as shining knights.
Manifesting political problems
to start up unnecessary fights.

Criminalising anyone who requests
or assists an abortion.
Not realising their hypocritical
manners of contortion.
Forcing women to bear children
has become a form of extortion.
Punishing her, without punishing him
is unjust apportion.

Going out of their way to maintain
their heroic deception.
By obstructing the media
with their falsified perception.
Convincing themselves
and the entirety of their nation.
That this is a much needed
form of regulation.

Under a Table

Isn't it funny…

How parents send their children
to gain an education.
Hoping to shape the minds
of the next generation.
Unaware of
the momentary desperation.
That these kids face
with the current legislation.

Being taught how best
to quickly hide under a table.
When they hear the gunshots
that the U.S. laws enable.
The news reports don't hesitate
to smack on a label.
For it was the fault
of the mentally unstable.

Don't expect the government
to claim any responsibility.
They'll argue it has nothing to do
with their capability.

Hosting Sagacity

Isn't it funny…

How this year's World Cup
has caused a lot of agitation.
By those who discriminate
against the hosting nation.
Highlighting their distaste
for Qatar's way of civilisation.
For it doesn't assimilate
to the Westernised Caucasian.

The Middle East will always
be under hostile examination.
By the same invading countries
that ran colonisation.
Don't bother asking them
for a logical explanation.
As to why they orchestrated
the ultimate rights violation.

And yet they still
possess the audacity.
To question Qatar's
hosting sagacity.
Get outta here
with that relentless voracity.
Motivated by none other
than the rapacity.

Intended Provocation

Isn't it funny...

How Europeans were so quick
to form an alliance.
Immediately after the alleged
displays of violence.
Not allowing themselves
to dismissively sit in silence.
For that would implicate
a betrayed sense of compliance.

The U.S won't own up
to their unwarranted instigation.
Knowing it would cause
the intended provocation.
Russia warned them
against the NATO continuation.
But the U.S persisted
on getting Ukraine's affiliation.

The U.S and Europe openly supported
Ukraine's resistance.
While aiding Israel in eradicating
Palestine's existence.
Forgive me as I sit back and laugh
at the lack of desistance.

Not the Monarchy

Isn't it funny…

How the British perceive themselves
as the epitome,
For having the only acceptable
form of civil liberty.

But was it not,
up until recently...
That the Queen died
and not the monarchy.

How can the invaded nations
be expected to commemorate,
The destruction and chaos
that Her Majesty helped facilitate.

Divide and Conquer

Isn't it funny…

How the West mocks
the Arab nations.
For having poor
Interrelations.
They refuse to acknowledge
their own contribution.
To the Middle East's
Border distribution.
If it wasn't for
the Western intrusion,
The Middle East
wouldn't need a "solution."

The methods used
to split up the land,
Was never considered
as something in-demand.
But of course,
it didn't matter...
The aim was to make
the civilisations scatter.

Colonise and vanquish.
Dethrone and banish.
Divide and conquer.
Makes it easier,
to take over.

Rumoured Atrocity

Isn't it funny…

How the news found photos and videos
of Israel killing Palestinians,
And then confidently reported it
as Russia attacking Ukrainians.

They really thought
we wouldn't notice.
That the media's sources
were completely bogus.
How they allowed them
to be shown as credible,
Has left me baffled.
It's incomprehensible.

To have to source outside
of the supposed attack,
Could it be they lied?
Am I a complete maniac
for finding it hard to believe
in what I'm expected to perceive.
This outrageous claim of monstrosity,
was it just a rumoured atrocity,
to gain the whole world's sympathy?

Unfamiliar Territory

Isn't it funny…

How they expect immigrants
and people of colour
to adapt to the laws
of a land full of flaws.
Otherwise
with zero hesitation,
they will be threatened
with deportation.

But when a white person
enters an unfamiliar territory,
They then feel entitled to complain
and enforce an unwanted campaign.
Simply because it doesn't conform
to their idolised Western norm.

You shouldn't travel to other nations
with your close-minded expectations.
Just because Qatar doesn't allow beer
in their stadiums,
Doesn't mean they are no longer
Homo sapiens.
Their laws
are different to yours.
They don't need
your deluded "cures."

Watching History Replicate

Isn't it funny…

How we look back and question
the Nazi's logic?
Why did the world allow them
to simply frolic?
The atrocities committed
are beyond comprehension.
Subjecting people through
undeserving reprehension.

You would hope for a better humanity,
one that isn't fuelled by brutality.
But rather, can act on rationality.
After learning about the fatality.

The Nazis attempted to cleanse
an entire race.
Simply because they didn't agree
with the Jewish faith.
The current world views this as
an inhumane disgrace.

But why does the world sit and wait,
until it's much too late
to spot the crimes of hate?
When they could have helped

to liberate,
Instead of watching history
replicate.

Another form of Nazi has risen.
Currently executing their mission.
While the world has made
a unanimous decision.
Knowing about the Uyghurs
and choosing not to listen.

Their "Service"

Isn't it funny…

How the US military is praised
for their "service"
When all they did
was cause a mess
and hurt us.

Ask yourselves,
what were they doing
invading other continents?
Why did they feel so inclined
to prove their dominance?

The U.S demonises the Soviet
while they bloody their hands
with no regret.
Expecting Americans
to eventually forget,
That they also oppose
a massive threat.

America should not
be pointing fingers
While the stench of
their history lingers.

Paradoxical Infliction

Isn't it funny…

How the British gave away land
that was never theirs.
Who gave them the right to meddle
with Palestine's affairs?
The Jews were welcomed
and given accommodation.
After having to deal with
their people's eradication.
Never did the Palestinians anticipate,
what the Zionists did to culminate…
The indisputable depiction,
of their paradoxical infliction.

Offering it to the Zionist agenda,
expecting the Palestinians
to simply surrender.
The British proposed
a "two-state solution"
But Palestine was never up
for distribution.
Forcing the division
and persecution,
Onto people
undeserving of diminution.

Normalising Segregation

Isn't it Funny…

How the world refuses
to engage in confrontation,
With France's blatant
religious discrimination.
They deserve nothing
but condemnation,
For all the hostile attempts
at normalising segregation.

They hate on the Muslims
and those who are black.
Speaking in their parliaments,
shouting to "go back."
This vile form of racism,
is in need of active criticism.
When will they finally be held liable,
For their acts have been unjustifiable.

Nakba

So long as there is confusion
About a situation
That requires your undivided attention
Allowing the oppressed
To go through the humiliation…

It shouldn't be so difficult
To understand the Palestinian retaliation.
What happened on Nakba Day
Lacked incitation.

The oppressed didn't fight back,
Not because they didn't want to.
But because the media
Works against them in every way.

They cannot stand,
They cannot say,
We were killed on this day.

Discarded

So long as there is confusion
About a situation
That requires a solution
But is treated as a delusion.

The people of Syria
were being bombarded
Their lifeless bodies
laid there, discarded.
The leaders of today
have abandoned you
They should consider themselves
blessed
For not experiencing
what you've had to go through.

They watched you bleed
As they sat amongst their riches.
For which they do not deserve.
They have grown selfish
And are controlled like bitches.
Not by their people,
For which they should serve.

Your children have stopped screaming.
They've also stopped crying.
You look around you and watch them,
As they lay there, dying.

Your pain is real,
And it's one worth acknowledgement.
The world remains convinced,
That they had no involvement.

They reject you from their country,
Claiming… how do I put this bluntly?
According to the hateful racist,
YOU are the terrorist.

Out of the Equation

So long as there is confusion
About a situation
Where freedom is an illusion.

Provided through taxation
By everyday workers
That can't go on vacation
As well as the homeless
That are going through starvation.

But let us continue
To sit back in formation
While we watch the variation
Of Australian leaders
That can't rule a nation.

Can I get a confirmation,
From the voting calculation...
Was I left out of the equation?

Regarding Immigration

So long as there is confusion
About a situation
Regarding immigration
Going through all that frustration

It's quite easy to ignore
The discrimination
When you are not the one
Facing deportation
We like to think
That segregation has ended
But we will never understand
How much it has offended

And yet we claim to be a democracy
Oh, what a world of hypocrisy
At least there is some form of consistency
Displayed by all the bigotry
Where is the human decency?

Same Creation

19

When there is no more confusion
About any situation...
We would have finally come to the realisation,
That we are all a part of the same creation.

Isn't it funny...

...?

www.ingramcontent.com/pod-product-compliance
Lightning Source LLC
La Vergne TN
LVHW021349200726

843509LV00014B/2753